THE
Junior Baker
COOKBOOK

DEVELOPED BY

WILLIAMS SONOMA

TEST KITCHEN

photographs Aubrie Pick

weldon**owen**

Contents

7 Let's Bake!

8 Preparing Equipment

11 Baker's Pantry

12 Recipes

70 Index

There's nothing like dessert warm from the oven! Head to page 52 to get the recipes for these Mini S'Mores Tarts.

Let's Bake!

Cookies, cakes, breads, and other delicious baked confections are the ultimate treats. Whether you're waking up with a coffee-cake muffin, enjoying an afternoon snack of perfect chocolate chip cookies, or serving buttermilk biscuits with dinner, there are so many ways to savor baked goods any time of day. And what's more, you can have a lot of fun learning to make these recipes from scratch! With the help of an adult, you can enjoy the satisfaction of mixing together a few simple ingredients to make unforgettable snacks and desserts. Don't forget to share!

This collection of easy-to-prepare recipes, a companion book to Williams Sonoma's popular Junior Chef cooking class series, will inspire you to explore and create in your own kitchen. You'll find recipes for making all your favorite confections from the bakery, like cinnamon rolls, shortbread, mini cupcakes, whoopee pies, brownies and blondies, cheesecake, biscotti, and many more. Discover savory breads, like dinner rolls with a homemade spice blend, pizza-like focaccia topped with tomatoes, and scones flavored with bacon and cheese.

Also included are plenty of tips, tricks, and solutions for simplifying recipes. A handy guide to preparing equipment, stocking basic ingredients, and testing for doneness will help you become a baking pro! Before you know it, your friends will be asking you to bake their birthday cakes—and you'll be ready to whip up a festive confetti cake. So crank up the oven, roll up your sleeves, and fill the kitchen with mouthwatering smells.

Preparing Equipment

Many recipes call for buttering, flouring, and/or lining baking equipment. Here's how to get it done:

- **Buttering:** Use a piece of wax paper to hold a pat of softened, unsalted butter and generously coat the pan's inside, bottom, and sides.

- **Buttering and Flouring:** Follow the buttering method above, then add 2 tablespoons flour to the pan. Tilt and shake the pan to coat the buttered surface evenly. Tap out any excess.

- **Lining Round Pans:** Butter (see above) the pan. Cut out a large sheet of parchment paper. Place the cake pan right side up on the parchment and trace the circumference. Cut out the circle just slightly to the inside of your traced line so that the parchment fits snugly in the pan bottom, not coming up the sides.

- **Lining Rimmed Baking Sheets:** Cut a piece of parchment paper about the length of the baking sheet. Place the parchment in the baking sheet, folding the excess until it fits snugly. Using the paper folds as your guide, use scissors to trim the parchment. Lay it in the baking sheet, making sure that it covers all the corners but does not fold over the sides.

> **Testing for Doneness** Most recipes include both a time and a visual cue to test for doneness. It's important to follow these instructions and to always set a timer! For most cakes, you can use a toothpick to check for doneness: When you think the cake is done, stick a clean toothpick into the center. If the toothpick comes out clean, the cake is ready. If the toothpick comes out with batter on it, the cake needs more baking.

Buttering pans helps stop food from sticking: foods release more easily and pans are easier to clean.

Baker's Pantry

A well-stocked pantry means being able to bake whenever a craving strikes with little need to plan or shop. Keep these essential baker's ingredients on hand, supplementing them with any special or fresh ingredients a recipe requires.

- **Flour:** There are many varieties of flour, but most of the recipes in this book call for all-purpose flour. Some brands offer bleached and unbleached versions of all-purpose flour. You can use either type for these recipes.

- **Baking Soda:** Cookie doughs and cake batters rely on this leavening agent to help them rise in the oven. Baking soda reacts immediately when mixed with liquid, so it should always be combined with dry ingredients before liquid is added.

- **Baking Powder:** This is another powerful leavening agent that, when mixed with liquid, releases carbon dioxide bubbles that give baked goods a fluffy, airy texture.

- **Eggs:** Fresh eggs are important for adding moisture to baked goods. Choose eggs labeled "medium" or "large"; using extra-large eggs can lead to doughs or batters that are too wet.

- **Vanilla Extract:** Look for pure vanilla extract at the store. Made from real vanilla beans, it costs more than the bottles labeled "imitation vanilla," but it has a purer, more complex flavor.

Swap It Out

Sometimes recipes call for ingredients that you either don't have or don't enjoy. Here's a simple key to swapping out ingredients.

Buttermilk: For every 1 cup of buttermilk called for, use 1 cup milk mixed with 1 tablespoon white wine vinegar or lemon juice. Let the mixture sit for a few minutes until it is slightly curdled.

Nuts and Dried Fruit: You can use any nut or dried fruit you like, just make sure it's a similar size to the original ingredient called for in the recipe. If not, chop it to match that size.

Eggs: In cake and quick bread batters, you can substitute ¼ cup applesauce or mashed banana (about half a banana) for every egg called for in the recipe.

Mixed Berry Mini Galettes

A galette is a free-form pie baked on a baking sheet rather than in a pie plate. The sugar and egg wash added at the end make the crust sparkle and shine.

1 To make the filling, in a bowl, stir together the berries, lemon juice, granulated sugar, and flour. Set aside.

2 To make the dough, whisk together the flour and salt. Using a food processor or pastry cutter, blend in the butter until the mixture resembles coarse sand. Add the water and blend until a dough forms.

3 Line a baking sheet with parchment paper. Turn the dough out onto a lightly floured work surface and roll out into a 16-by-12-inch rectangle about ¼ inch thick. Using a 6-inch round cutter, cut out 4 rounds of dough. Transfer to the prepared baking sheet.

4 In a small bowl, whisk together the egg and 1 teaspoon water. Brush the edges of the dough rounds with some of the egg mixture. Divide the filling evenly among the rounds, placing it in a mound in the center. Fold the edges of the dough together up and over the filling, forming loose pleats and leaving the center uncovered. Brush the dough with the egg mixture and sprinkle with turbinado sugar. Refrigerate the galettes for at least 15 minutes or up to 4 hours.

5 Preheat the oven to 425°F. Bake until the dough is golden brown and the filling is bubbling, about 25 minutes. Have an adult help you transfer the baking sheet to a wire rack and let the galettes cool slightly. Serve the galettes warm or at room temperature, topped with whipped cream, if desired.

For the filling

3 cups mixed fresh berries, such as blackberries, raspberries, blueberries, and thinly sliced strawberries

2 tablespoons fresh lemon juice

¼ cup granulated sugar

¼ cup all-purpose flour

For the dough

2 cups all-purpose flour, plus more for dusting

½ teaspoon kosher salt

¾ cup cold unsalted butter, cut into cubes

⅓ cup very cold water

1 large egg

Turbinado sugar, for sprinkling

Whipped Cream (page 65), for serving (optional)

For an extra-chocolaty loaf, substitute ¼ cup unsweetened cocoa powder for ¼ cup of the all-purpose flour.

Chocolate Banana Loaf Bread

This delicious loaf is an example of a "quick" bread, which uses fast-acting baking powder and baking soda, rather than slow-acting yeast, to make the batter rise. Perfect for both breakfasts and snacks, it will disappear quickly too!

1 Preheat the oven to 350°F. Butter and lightly flour a 9-by-5-inch loaf pan or three 6-by-3½-inch mini loaf pans.

2 In a bowl, sift together the flour, baking soda, baking powder, and salt. Set aside.

3 In the bowl of a stand mixer fitted with the paddle attachment, beat together the butter and sugar on medium speed until light and fluffy, about 3 minutes. Add the eggs 1 at a time, then the vanilla, and beat until combined, about 1 minute.

4 Reduce the speed to low, add the bananas, and beat until combined, about 30 seconds. Add the flour mixture and beat just until the flour disappears. Stop the mixer and use a rubber spatula to gently fold in the chocolate chips until evenly distributed. Pour the batter into the prepared pan(s) and smooth the top. Sprinkle with chocolate chips.

5 Bake until the bread is golden brown and a toothpick inserted into the center comes out clean, 50-60 minutes for the large loaf and about 35 minutes for the mini loaves. Have an adult help you transfer the pan(s) to a wire rack and let cool for 15 minutes. Turn the bread out onto the rack and let cool completely before slicing. Store wrapped in plastic wrap or aluminum foil at room temperature for up to 3 days or in the refrigerator for up to 1 week.

½ cup unsalted butter, at room temperature, plus more for the pan

1¾ cups all-purpose flour, plus more for dusting

1 teaspoon baking soda

½ teaspoon baking powder

¼ teaspoon kosher salt

1 cup sugar

2 large eggs

1 teaspoon vanilla extract

3 very ripe bananas, mashed (about 1½ cups)

½ cup semisweet chocolate chips, plus more for sprinkling

Cinnamon Monkey Bread

Serve this treat warm from the oven and watch everyone have fun pulling the bread apart. If you don't have a Bundt pan, you can use an angel food cake pan or a tube pan—the central tube helps the bread bake evenly.

1 To make the dough, in a large measuring cup, combine the milk and yeast and stir once to combine. Let stand until foamy and fragrant, 3–5 minutes.

2 In the bowl of a stand mixer fitted with the paddle attachment, beat together the flour, granulated sugar, and salt on low speed just until the flour disappears, about 1 minute. Add the melted butter and vanilla and beat until combined, about 2 minutes. Pour in the yeast mixture and beat on low speed until the dough just begins to come together, about 1–2 minutes. Switch to the dough hook and beat on medium speed until the dough is shiny and smooth, 7–8 minutes.

3 Turn the dough out onto a lightly floured work surface and knead the dough a few times, then form into a ball. Transfer the dough to a lightly oiled bowl, lightly coat the top of the dough with nonstick cooking spray, and cover with plastic wrap. Let the dough rise in a warm spot until doubled in size, about 1½ hours.

4 Meanwhile, make the topping: Place the melted butter in a medium bowl. In another medium bowl, stir together the brown sugar and cinnamon.

For the dough

1½ cups warm whole milk (115°F–120°F)

2¼ teaspoons active dry yeast

3¼ cups all-purpose flour, plus more for dusting

¼ cup plus 2 tablespoons granulated sugar

1½ teaspoons kosher salt

2 tablespoons unsalted butter, melted and cooled, plus butter for the pan

3 teaspoons vanilla extract

Nonstick cooking spray

For the topping

¾ cup unsalted butter, melted

1½ cups firmly packed light brown sugar

2 tablespoons ground cinnamon

5 Generously butter a 15-cup Bundt pan. Turn the dough out onto a lightly floured surface and gently pat into an 8-inch square. Using a lightly floured pastry cutter or knife, cut the dough into 64 pieces, each about 1 inch square. Roll each piece into a ball, then dip in the melted butter and roll in the brown sugar mixture. Layer the balls in the prepared pan: be sure to stagger the balls instead of stacking them on top of each other to help the bread to bake together into a puzzle shape.

6 Cover the pan tightly with plastic wrap. Let the dough rise in a warm spot until the balls are puffy and have risen at least 1 inch above the top of the pan, about 1 hour.

7 Preheat the oven to 350°F. Remove the plastic wrap from the pan. Bake until the sugar caramelizes and the dough balls are firm to the touch, about 30 minutes. Have an adult help you transfer the pan to a wire rack and let cool for only 5 minutes, then invert the bread onto a serving plate. Let cool for 8–10 minutes.

8 Meanwhile, make the glaze: In a small bowl, whisk together the confectioners' sugar, milk, vanilla, and salt until smooth. Pour the glaze over the warm bread and serve warm.

. . . .

For the glaze

½ cup confectioners' sugar

1 tablespoon whole milk

¼ teaspoon vanilla extract

Pinch of kosher salt

Don't let the bread cool in the pan for more than 5 minutes or it will stick to the pan and come out in pieces.

Perfect Chocolate Chip Cookies

Make this recipe your own by adding a handful of dried fruit, like cherries or cranberries, or chopped nuts, such as walnuts or pecans, to the cookie dough when you add the chocolate chips.

1 Preheat the oven to 350°F. Line a baking sheet with parchment paper.

2 In a bowl, sift together the flour, baking soda, and kosher salt. Set aside.

3 In the bowl of a stand mixer fitted with the paddle attachment, beat together the butter and both sugars on medium speed until light and fluffy, about 3 minutes. Reduce the speed to low, add the egg, then the egg yolks and vanilla, and beat until combined, about 1 minute. Stop the mixer and scrape down the sides of the bowl.

4 Add the flour mixture and beat on low speed just until the flour disappears, about 1 minute. Stop the mixer and use a rubber spatula to fold in the chocolate until evenly distributed.

5 Drop the dough by rounded tablespoonfuls onto the prepared baking sheet, spacing the cookies about 1 inch apart. Sprinkle the top of the cookies with sea salt.

6 Bake until the cookies are golden brown, 8–10 minutes. Place the baking sheet on a wire rack and let cool for about 3 minutes, then transfer the cookies to a wire rack and let cool slightly before serving. Store in an airtight container at room temperature for up to 5 days. See page 68 for a Salted Caramel Chocolate Chip Cookie variation.

2¼ cups all-purpose flour

1 teaspoon baking soda

1 teaspoon kosher salt

1 cup unsalted butter, at room temperature

⅔ cup granulated sugar

⅔ cup firmly packed light brown sugar

1 large egg plus 2 large egg yolks

2 teaspoons vanilla extract

¾ lb semisweet chocolate, chopped into ½-inch chunks

Sea salt, for sprinkling

Coffee-Cake Muffins

Streusel is a traditional topping on many German desserts. Experiment with adding streusel to other desserts, like the Mixed Berry Mini Galettes (page 12).

1 Preheat the oven to 350°F. Line 12 standard muffin cups with paper liners.

2 To make the streusel, in a bowl, whisk together the flour, brown sugar, and cinnamon. Using clean fingers, mix in the butter until the streusel is moist and crumbly; don't overmix. Set aside.

3 To make the muffins, in another bowl, whisk together the flour, baking powder, baking soda, and salt. Set aside.

4 In the bowl of a stand mixer fitted with the paddle attachment, beat together the butter and granulated sugar on medium speed until light and fluffy, about 3 minutes. Add the eggs 1 at a time and beat until incorporated, about 1 minute. Add the vanilla and beat until combined, about 30 seconds. Reduce the speed to low, add the sour cream, milk, and flour mixture and beat until combined, about 1 minute.

5 Divide half of the batter among the prepared muffin cups and sprinkle with half of the streusel, then repeat with the remaining batter and streusel.

6 Bake until the streusel is crispy and lightly browned and a toothpick inserted into the center of a muffin comes out clean, 25–30 minutes. Have an adult help you transfer the pan to a wire rack to let cool slightly, then turn the muffins out onto the rack to cool completely before serving. Store in an airtight container at room temperature for up to 3 days.

For the streusel

½ cup all-purpose flour

½ cup firmly packed dark brown sugar

3 teaspoons ground cinnamon

5 tablespoons unsalted butter, at room temperature

For the muffins

2¼ cups all-purpose flour

2 teaspoons baking powder

½ teaspoon baking soda

⅛ teaspoon kosher salt

½ cup plus 3 tablespoons unsalted butter, at room temperature

1 cup granulated sugar

2 large eggs

1 teaspoon vanilla extract

1 cup sour cream

3 tablespoons whole milk

Vanilla Cheesecake with Strawberries

In winter, when sweet strawberries are hard to find, try topping the cake with juicy citrus like blood oranges or Meyer lemons. Trim off the peel and the white pith before cutting out each segment for a pretty presentation.

1 To make the crust, preheat the oven to 350°F. In a large bowl, stir together the graham crackers, melted butter, sugar, and salt. Press the mixture evenly into the bottom and 1 inch up the sides of a 9-inch springform pan. Bake until the crust is lightly browned and set, about 8 minutes. Have an adult help you transfer the pan to a wire rack and let cool completely. Reduce the oven temperature to 325°F.

2 To make the filling, in the bowl of a stand mixer fitted with the paddle attachment, beat the cream cheese on medium-high speed until smooth, about 2 minutes. Add the eggs 1 at a time, then the sugar, vanilla, lemon juice, and salt, and beat until well combined, about 2 minutes. Add the sour cream, 1 cup at a time, and beat until combined, about 2 minutes. Stop the mixer to scrape down the sides of the bowl as needed. Pour the filling into the cooled crust and smooth the top.

3 Bake until the cheesecake is golden and the edges are firm but the center still jiggles, about 1 hour. Have an adult help you transfer the pan to a wire rack and let cool completely. Cover and refrigerate for at least 2 hours or up to overnight.

4 Loosen the clasp on the pan sides and remove the sides. With the help of a spatula, transfer the cheesecake to a plate. Just before serving, spread the whipped cream over the top and garnish with the strawberries.

For the crust

12 graham crackers, finely crushed

6 tablespoons unsalted butter, melted and cooled

¼ cup sugar

Pinch of kosher salt

For the filling

2 packages (½ lb each) cream cheese, at room temperature

3 large eggs

1¼ cups sugar

2 teaspoons vanilla extract

1 tablespoon fresh lemon juice

Pinch of kosher salt

2 cups sour cream

Whipped Cream (page 65), for serving

Strawberry Topping (page 68)

If the cheesecake sticks to the pan, gently run a knife around the edge to loosen the cake before releasing.

Madeleines

Buttery French treats that are not too sweet, these madeleines are also delicious dipped in chocolate. To do that, follow the steps in the Chocolate Almond Orange Biscotti recipe (page 48).

makes
12
MADELEINES

1 Preheat the oven to 375°F. Lightly butter a 12-mold madeleine pan.

2 In a small bowl, sift together the flour, baking powder, and salt. Set aside.

3 In the bowl of a stand mixer fitted with the whisk attachment, beat together the eggs and granulated sugar on high speed until pale and thick, about 3 minutes. Add the vanilla and lemon zest and beat until combined, about 1 minute. Reduce the speed to low, add the flour mixture, and beat just until the flour mixture disappears, about 2 minutes. Stop the mixer and scrape down the sides of the bowl. Gently fold in half of the melted butter until just blended, then fold in the remaining butter.

4 Spoon a heaping tablespoonful of batter into each prepared mold. Bake until the edges of the madeleines are golden brown and the tops are domed, 8–10 minutes; halfway through baking, have an adult help you rotate the pan 180 degrees.

5 Have an adult help you remove the pan from the oven, and let the madeleines cool in the pan for 10 minutes, then carefully invert the pan and tap to release the madeleines onto a wire rack. Let cool completely. Using a fine-mesh sieve or a sifter, dust the madeleines with confectioners' sugar, if desired. Store in an airtight container at room temperature for up to 2 days.

4 tablespoons unsalted butter, melted and cooled, plus butter for the pan

½ cup all-purpose flour

½ teaspoon baking powder

¼ teaspoon kosher salt

2 large eggs

⅓ cup granulated sugar

½ teaspoon vanilla extract

1 teaspoon grated lemon zest

Confectioners' sugar, for dusting (optional)

Cookies & Cream Mini Cupcakes

Miniature cookies make a crunchy garnish for these adorable cupcakes, which are as fun to eat as they are to make. If you don't have a mini muffin tin, use a regular muffin tin—just add a few minutes to the baking time.

1 Preheat the oven to 350°F. Line 24 mini muffin cups with paper liners or coat with nonstick cooking spray.

2 In a bowl, sift together the flour, baking powder, and salt. Set aside.

3 In the bowl of a stand mixer fitted with the paddle attachment, beat together the butter and sugar on medium speed until light and fluffy, about 3 minutes. Add the eggs 1 at a time, then the vanilla, and beat until combined, about 1 minute.

4 Reduce the speed to low and add the flour mixture in 2 additions, alternating with the milk, and beat just until the flour mixture disappears, about 30 seconds. Stop the mixer and use a rubber spatula to fold in the crushed cookies until well combined. Divide the batter among the prepared muffin cups, filling them no more than three-fourths full.

5 Bake until a toothpick inserted into the center of a cupcake comes out clean, about 12 minutes. Have an adult help you transfer the pan to a wire rack and let cool for 5 minutes, then transfer the cupcakes to the rack and let cool completely.

6 Using a small icing spatula or a butter knife, frost the cupcakes as desired. Garnish each cupcake with a chocolate cookie wedge. Store in an airtight container at room temperature for up to 1 day or in the refrigerator for up to 1 week.

Nonstick cooking spray (optional)

1½ cups all-purpose flour

1½ teaspoons baking powder

¼ teaspoon kosher salt

½ cup unsalted butter, at room temperature

¾ cup sugar

2 large eggs

1½ teaspoons vanilla extract

¾ cup whole milk

1 cup crushed chocolate sandwich cookies

Cookies & Cream Frosting (page 65)

Wedges of chocolate sandwich cookies, for garnish

To make mini round
pies, use ¼ cup filling,
then top with a second
dough round and
crimp the edges.

Apple Hand Pies

Hand pies are built to eat on the go, making them a great choice to include in lunch boxes or take along on a hike. Experiment with adding a handful of raisins or dried cranberries to the apple mixture.

1 Make the dough. In a saucepan, stir together the apples, brown sugar, cinnamon, salt, and vanilla. Place over medium heat and cook, stirring occasionally, until the apples are tender, about 10 minutes. Stir in the flour and cook, stirring occasionally, until the flour is absorbed, about 3 minutes. Let cool to room temperature.

2 Remove the dough from the plastic wrap. On a lightly floured work surface, roll out the dough about ⅛ inch thick into a 12-by-18-inch rectangle. Using a 4-inch round cutter, cut out 16 rounds, gathering up the scraps of dough and rerolling as needed.

3 In a small bowl, whisk together the egg and milk. Brush the edges of the dough rounds with some of the egg mixture. Place about 2 tablespoons of the apple filling in the center of each round, then fold over to form a half-moon. Seal the edges and crimp them with the tines of a fork. Cut a small slit in the top of each pie. Brush the tops of the pies with the egg mixture and sprinkle with turbinado sugar. Refrigerate for 30 minutes.

4 Meanwhile, preheat the oven to 375°F. Place the pies on a baking sheet lined with parchment paper. Bake until the pies are golden brown, about 20 minutes. Have an adult help you remove the baking sheet from the oven and transfer the pies to a wire rack and let cool to room temperature before serving.

Cream Cheese Dough
(page 66)

1 lb apples, such as Fuji or Pink Lady, peeled, cored, and cut into ¼-inch cubes

2 tablespoons firmly packed light brown sugar

½ teaspoon ground cinnamon

¼ teaspoon kosher salt

1 teaspoon vanilla extract

1 tablespoon all-purpose flour, plus more for dusting

1 large egg

1 teaspoon whole milk

Turbinado sugar, for sprinkling

Red Velvet Cupcakes

Have you ever made a volcano using baking soda and vinegar? Mixed together, the two ingredients create a fizzy reaction that helps to make these delicious cupcakes light and airy.

1 Preheat the oven to 350°F. Line 24 standard muffin cups with paper liners or coat with nonstick cooking spray.

2 In a bowl, sift together the flour, cocoa powder, baking soda, baking powder, and salt. In a small bowl, whisk together the buttermilk, food coloring, and vinegar. Set both bowls aside.

3 In the bowl of a stand mixer fitted with the paddle attachment, beat together the butter and sugar on medium speed until light and fluffy, about 3 minutes. Add the eggs 1 at a time, then the vanilla, and beat until combined, about 1 minute.

4 Reduce the speed to low and add the flour mixture in 2 additions, alternating with the buttermilk mixture, and beat just until the flour mixture disappears, about 30 seconds. Divide the batter among the prepared muffin cups, filling them no more than halfway full.

5 Bake until a toothpick inserted into the center of a cupcake comes out clean, 18–20 minutes. Have an adult help you transfer the pan to a wire rack and let cool for 5 minutes, then remove the cupcakes from the pan and let cool completely on the rack.

6 Using a small icing spatula or a butter knife, frost the cupcakes as desired. Store the cupcakes in an airtight container at room temperature for up to 1 day or in the refrigerator for up to 1 week.

Nonstick cooking spray (optional)

2 cups plus 2 tablespoons all-purpose flour

2 tablespoons unsweetened cocoa powder

1 teaspoon baking soda

½ teaspoon baking powder

½ teaspoon kosher salt

1 cup buttermilk

1 tablespoon red food coloring

1 teaspoon white vinegar

½ cup unsalted butter, at room temperature

1½ cups sugar

2 large eggs, at room temperature

2 teaspoons vanilla extract

2 recipes Cream Cheese Frosting (page 65)

Be careful when adding the red food coloring, as it will stain counters and clothes!

Banana-Butterscotch Pie

If you add raw eggs directly to a hot mixture, the eggs will scramble. To prevent this, "temper" the eggs by whisking a small amount of the hot liquid into them before combining the two mixtures.

1 To make the crust, preheat the oven to 350°F. In a large bowl, stir together the graham crackers, melted butter, sugar, and salt. Press the mixture evenly into the bottom and up the sides of a 9-inch pie dish. Bake until the crust is lightly browned and set, about 8 minutes. Have an adult help you transfer the pan to a wire rack and let cool completely.

2 To make the filling, in another large bowl, whisk together the cornstarch and ½ cup of the milk. Let stand for 3 minutes, then whisk again. Add the eggs, egg yolks, and vanilla and whisk to combine. Set aside.

3 In a large saucepan over medium heat, combine the brown sugar, butter, and the remaining 2½ cups milk. Cook, stirring occasionally, until the milk just begins to simmer and the butter melts, about 5 minutes. Remove from the heat. Add ½ cup of the egg mixture to the milk mixture and whisk to combine. While whisking constantly, drizzle the hot milk mixture into the remaining egg mixture, then quickly pour the mixture into the saucepan. Cook over medium heat, whisking constantly, until tiny bubbles form and the mixture has thickened and darkened slightly, about 5 minutes. Strain the filling into a medium bowl. Let cool completely.

4 Pour the filling into the pie shell. Just before serving, spread the whipped cream in an even layer on top. In a medium bowl, stir together the bananas and brown sugar. Arrange the bananas around the outside pie edge.

For the crust

10 graham crackers, finely crushed

5 tablespoons unsalted butter, melted and cooled

3 tablespoons granulated sugar

Pinch of kosher salt

For the filling

½ cup cornstarch

3 cups whole milk

2 large eggs plus 2 large egg yolks

4 teaspoons vanilla extract

1¼ cups firmly packed light brown sugar

4 tablespoons unsalted butter

Whipped Cream (page 65)

2 bananas, cut into ¼-inch slices

2 tablespoons firmly packed light brown sugar

Nutella Brownies

Need to whip up a dessert in a hurry? This recipe comes together quickly and is yet another reason to make sure you always have a big jar of Nutella in your pantry.

1 Preheat the oven to 350°F. Line an 8-inch square baking dish with parchment paper, letting the paper overhang by about 2 inches on 2 opposite sides. Butter the parchment paper (but not the overhang) and the sides of the pan.

2 In the bowl of a stand mixer fitted with the paddle attachment, beat together the butter and brown sugar on medium speed until light and fluffy, about 3 minutes. Add the eggs 1 at a time, then the vanilla, and beat until combined, about 2 minutes. Add 1 cup of the Nutella and beat until well combined, about 1 minute.

3 Remove the bowl from the mixer. Sift the flour and salt over the butter mixture. Using a rubber spatula, fold until only a few streaks of flour remain. Stir in the chocolate chips until evenly distributed. Pour the batter into the prepared pan, then drop small spoonfuls of the remaining ½ cup Nutella evenly over the surface. Using a toothpick, draw circular patterns in the Nutella to swirl it into the batter.

4 Bake until a toothpick inserted into the center of the brownie comes out with a few moist crumbs attached, 30–35 minutes.

5 Have an adult help you transfer the pan to a wire rack to cool completely. Using the parchment overhang, remove the brownie from the pan, transfer to a cutting board, and slice into 2-inch squares. Store brownies in an airtight container at room temperature for up to 3 days.

5 tablespoons unsalted butter, at room temperature, plus more for the pan

½ cup plus 2 tablespoons firmly packed light brown sugar

2 large eggs

2 teaspoons vanilla extract

1½ cups Nutella

¾ cup all-purpose flour

½ teaspoon kosher salt

1 cup semisweet chocolate chips

31

Raspberry Swirled Meringues

These pretty pink treats are surprisingly easy to make. Save the leftover yolks to whip up a decadent omelet or luscious batch of French toast.

1 Preheat the oven to 325°F. Line 2 baking sheets with parchment paper.

2 In a blender, combine the raspberries and the 2 tablespoons sugar and purée until smooth, 1–2 minutes, stopping the blender to scrape down the sides as needed. Pour the purée through a fine-mesh sieve into a small bowl, using the back of a wooden spoon to press the purée through the sieve.

3 In the bowl of a stand mixer fitted with the whisk attachment, beat the egg whites on medium speed until foamy, about 1 minute. Add the cream of tartar and salt, raise the speed to high, and add the remaining 1 cup sugar, 1 tablespoon at a time. Beat until the egg whites hold stiff, glossy peaks, 5–7 minutes.

4 Stop the mixer and use a rubber spatula to gently fold ¼ cup of the raspberry purée into the meringue until lightly swirled. Spoon the meringue onto the prepared baking sheets, making mounds about 4 inches wide. Then spoon ½ teaspoon raspberry purée on top of each meringue and swirl with a toothpick.

5 Bake until the edges are just beginning to set, about 5 minutes. Reduce the oven temperature to 250°F and bake until the meringues are firm and just beginning to brown, about 45 minutes longer. Have an adult help you transfer the baking sheet to a wire rack and let the meringues cool completely on the sheet. Store in an airtight container for up to 3 days.

10 oz frozen raspberries

2 tablespoons plus
1 cup sugar

4 large egg whites

½ teaspoon cream
of tartar

¼ teaspoon kosher salt

Millionaire's Shortbread

makes **20** BARS

If you have a jar of extra-special sea salt in your pantry, this is the time to use it. Take these decadent bars over the top by finishing them with a sprinkle of delicate fleur de sel or pink Himalayan salt.

1 To make the crust, preheat the oven to 350°F. Line a 9-inch baking dish with aluminum foil, pushing it into the corners and letting the foil overhang by about 2 inches on 2 opposite sides. Repeat with the other side of the dish. Butter the foil.

2 In a food processor, combine the flour, brown sugar, cornstarch, and salt and pulse until blended. Add the butter and process until the mixture resembles coarse sand. Add the cold water and egg yolk and process until moist clumps form and the dough just begins to come together.

3 Transfer the dough to the prepared pan and press evenly into the bottom of the pan. Pierce the dough all over with a fork and bake until golden brown, about 20 minutes. Have an adult help you transfer the pan to a wire rack and let cool slightly.

continued on the next page

For the crust

½ cup cold unsalted butter, cut into cubes, plus butter for the dish

1 cup all-purpose flour

¼ cup firmly packed dark brown sugar

2½ teaspoons cornstarch

½ teaspoon kosher salt

2 tablespoons cold water

1 large egg yolk

4 To make the caramel, in a medium saucepan, whisk together the condensed milk and brown sugar. Add the butter, corn syrup, vanilla, and salt. Place over medium heat and bring to a gentle boil. Cook, whisking constantly, until the mixture has darkened slightly, is thickened, and reaches 220°F on a candy thermometer, 7–10 minutes. If the caramel begins to scorch, reduce the heat. Carefully pour the caramel over the warm crust and let cool until set, about 20 minutes.

5 To make the chocolate topping, in a microwave-safe bowl, combine the chocolate and cream. Microwave in 30-second increments, stirring in between, until the chocolate is almost completely melted, then stir until smooth. Pour the chocolate over the set caramel, spread in an even layer, and let cool slightly. Sprinkle sea salt over the chocolate, if desired.

6 Cover the dessert with plastic wrap and refrigerate until firm, at least 2 hours or up to overnight. Use the foil to lift the dessert from the pan, transfer to a cutting board, and cut into squares. Store in an airtight container in the refrigerator for up to 3 days.

For the caramel

1 can (14 oz) sweetened condensed milk

½ cup plus 2 tablespoons firmly packed dark brown sugar

7 tablespoons unsalted butter, cut into pieces

2 tablespoons light corn syrup

1½ teaspoons vanilla extract

½ teaspoon kosher salt

For the chocolate topping

1½ cups semisweet chocolate chips

¼ cup heavy cream

Sea salt, for sprinkling (optional)

Chocolate Tart with Crushed Hazelnuts

"Blind baking" is a technique for baking a pie or tart crust separately from its filling. If you use dried beans as pie weights, save them to use again for baking but don't cook with them—the time in the oven dries them out.

1 Make the tart crust. Preheat the oven to 325°F. In a large heatproof bowl, combine the chocolate, cream, butter, and salt and set over a saucepan of simmering water, making sure that the water isn't touching the bottom of the bowl. Heat, stirring occasionally, until the chocolate and butter melt, about 5 minutes. Remove the bowl from the heat and stir to combine. Whisk in the eggs, egg yolks, brown sugar, and vanilla until smooth. Set aside.

2 Remove the tart crust from the freezer. Line the inside of the crust with aluminum foil or parchment paper and fill with pie weights or dried beans. Bake until it looks set, about 20 minutes. Have an adult help you remove the pan from the oven and carefully remove the foil and weights.

3 Pour the chocolate mixture into the warm crust and sprinkle the hazelnuts over the top. Bake until the filling is set, 15–20 minutes. Have an adult help you remove the pan from the oven and let the tart cool on a wire rack slightly before serving, or let cool completely, then cover and refrigerate for up to 2 days.

4 Just before serving, top the tart with whipped cream or, using a fine-mesh sieve or a sifter, dust with confectioners' sugar.

Chocolate Tart Dough (page 67)

½ lb semisweet chocolate, coarsely chopped, or 1½ cups semisweet chocolate chips

2 tablespoons heavy cream

6 tablespoons unsalted butter

½ teaspoon kosher salt

2 large eggs plus 2 large egg yolks

½ cup firmly packed light brown sugar

2 teaspoons vanilla extract

¼ cup hazelnuts, roughly chopped

Whipped Cream (page 65) or confectioners' sugar, for serving

37

Brown Butter Rice Krispy Treats

Once you've tried our version of this classic treat, you'll never follow the back of the cereal box again! The subtle flavors of brown butter and sea salt will be popular with adults and kids alike.

1 Place a rack in the upper third of the oven and preheat to 375°F. Line a baking sheet with parchment paper. Coat an 8-inch square baking dish with nonstick cooking spray, then line the bottom with parchment paper and coat the parchment.

2 Place the marshmallows in a single layer on the prepared baking sheet and bake until toasted, 6–8 minutes. Set aside.

3 In a large saucepan over medium heat, melt the butter. Reduce the heat to medium-low and simmer gently, swirling the pan often, until the butter is toasty brown and smells nutty, about 5 minutes. Watch carefully at the end to prevent the butter from burning. Add the marshmallows and stir until melted, about 2 minutes.

4 Remove the pan from the heat and stir in the vanilla. Add the crispy rice cereal and stir until well coated. Transfer the mixture to the prepared baking dish and spread in an even layer, pressing down to compact slightly. Sprinkle with sea salt. Let stand until set, about 15 minutes, then cut into 1½-inch squares. Store in an airtight container at room temperature for up to 2 days.

Nonstick cooking spray

1 lb marshmallows

5 tablespoons unsalted butter

½ teaspoon vanilla extract

6 cups crispy rice cereal

Flaky sea salt, for sprinkling

Brown Sugar Blondies

makes · 12-16 · BARS

The white chocolate chips in these bars set them apart from other blondie recipes. For a different taste treat, try substituting butterscotch chips for the white chocolate and adding a handful of shredded coconut.

1 Preheat the oven to 350°F. Butter an 8-inch square baking dish.

2 In a bowl, sift together the flour, baking powder, and salt. Set aside.

3 In the bowl of a stand mixer fitted with the paddle attachment, beat together the butter, brown sugar, and vanilla on medium speed until light and fluffy, about 3 minutes. Reduce the speed to low and add the eggs 1 at a time, beating well after each addition. Raise the speed to medium-high and beat until very fluffy, about 2 minutes. Stop the mixer and scrape down the sides of the bowl.

4 Add the flour mixture and beat on low speed just until the flour mixture disappears, about 1 minute. Stop the mixer and use a rubber spatula to fold in the white chocolate chips until just blended. Scrape the batter into the prepared pan and spread evenly.

5 Bake until a toothpick inserted into the center of the blondie comes out clean, 25–30 minutes. Have an adult help you transfer the pan to a wire rack and let cool completely. Cut into bars and serve. Store blondies in an airtight container at room temperature for up to 3 days. See page 68 for a Brown Butter & Hazelnut Blondie variation.

¾ cup unsalted butter, at room temperature, plus more for the dish

1¼ cups all-purpose flour

1 teaspoon baking powder

¼ teaspoon kosher salt

1 cup firmly packed light brown sugar

1 teaspoon vanilla extract

2 large eggs

¼ cup white chocolate chips

Confetti Birthday Cake

This festive cake has double the sprinkles for double the fun.
Use a serrated knife to trim off the rounded top of each cake layer
to create a flat surface for icing. The baker gets the trimmings!

1 Preheat the oven to 325°F. Lightly butter three 8-inch round cake pans, line the bottom with parchment paper, and butter the parchment. Dust with flour, tapping out any excess flour.

2 In a large bowl, sift together the flour, baking powder, baking soda, and salt. In a large liquid measuring cup, whisk together the whole milk, buttermilk, and water. Set aside. In the bowl of a stand mixer fitted with the paddle attachment, beat the butter on medium speed until smooth, about 3 minutes. Add the sugar and vanilla and beat until light and fluffy, about 2 minutes. Add the eggs 1 at a time and beat until incorporated, about 1 minute.

3 Add the flour mixture in 4 additions, alternating with the milk mixture and beginning and ending with the flour mixture, and beat just until the flour mixture disappears, about 2 minutes. Stop the mixer after each addition to scrape down the sides of the bowl. Then stop the mixer and use a rubber spatula to gently fold in 1 cup of the sprinkles. Divide the batter evenly among the prepared pans and smooth the tops.

continued on the next page

1 cup unsalted butter, at room temperature, plus more for the pans

3¼ cups all-purpose flour, plus more for the pans

1 tablespoon baking powder

1 teaspoon baking soda

¾ teaspoon kosher salt

¾ cup whole milk

½ cup buttermilk

¾ cup cold water

1¾ cups sugar

1 tablespoon vanilla extract

3 large eggs

2 cups rainbow sprinkles

Buttercream Frosting (page 66)

41

4 Bake until a toothpick inserted into the center of the cakes comes out clean, about 40 minutes. Have an adult help you transfer the pans to wire racks and let cool for 20 minutes, then invert the cakes onto the racks and let cool completely. Using a serrated knife, trim off the rounded tops to make the cakes flat on both sides.

5 To assemble the cake, place the bottom cake layer on a plate, top side up, and using an offset spatula or a butter knife, spread one-third of the frosting over the top. Place the second cake layer on top, also top side up, and spread half of the remaining frosting over the top. Repeat with the third cake layer and remaining frosting. Decorate with the remaining 1 cup sprinkles. Store the cake wrapped tightly in plastic wrap in the refrigerator for up to 2 days.

Dried Cherry & Almond Mini Scones

makes about
18
SCONES

To knead the dough into a ball, sprinkle it with flour, fold it in half over itself, and press the halves together. Then pick up the dough, give it a quarter turn, and repeat the folding.

1 Preheat the oven to 400°F. Line a baking sheet with parchment paper.

2 In a food processor, combine the flour, granulated sugar, baking powder, baking soda, salt, and cinnamon and pulse until blended. Add the butter and process until the mixture resembles coarse sand. In a small bowl, whisk together the egg, buttermilk, and almond extract. With the processor running, add the egg mixture in a slow, steady stream and process until the dough just comes together. Transfer the dough to a large bowl and fold in the dried cherries and almonds.

3 Turn the dough out onto a floured work surface and knead once or twice, then shape the dough into a ball. Roll out the dough into a 12-by-8-inch rectangle about ½ inch thick. Using a 2-inch round cutter, cut out as many scones as you can and transfer to the prepared baking sheet, spacing the scones about 3 inches apart. Gather the scraps into a ball, roll out the dough again, and cut out more scones. Be sure not to reroll the dough more than once.

4 Bake until the scones are golden brown, about 12 minutes. Have an adult help you transfer the scones to a wire rack and let cool.

5 In a small bowl, whisk together the confectioners' sugar and milk to form a thick glaze, adding more milk a little at a time as needed. Dip the top of each scone into the glaze and garnish with almonds. Store the scones in an airtight container at room temperature for up to 3 days.

2 cups all-purpose flour, plus more for dusting

1 tablespoon granulated sugar

2 teaspoons baking powder

½ teaspoon baking soda

¼ teaspoon kosher salt

1 teaspoon ground cinnamon

½ cup cold unsalted butter, cut into cubes

1 large egg

¾ cup buttermilk

1 teaspoon almond extract

⅓ cup dried cherries

⅓ cup slivered almonds, plus more for garnish

½ cup confectioners' sugar

1 teaspoon whole milk, plus more as needed

43

Pumpkin Whoopie Pies

Serve these delectable treats, full of the flavors of fall, with a steaming mug of hot apple cider or herbal tea, garnished with a cinnamon stick.

1 Preheat the oven to 350°F. Line 2 baking sheets with parchment paper.

2 In a medium bowl, whisk together the flour, salt, baking powder, baking soda, cinnamon, ginger, and cloves. Set aside.

3 In a large bowl, whisk together the pumpkin purée, oil, egg, vanilla, and brown sugar. Sprinkle the flour mixture over the pumpkin mixture and whisk just until the flour mixture disappears. Place a large disposable pastry bag in a container or drinking glass. Pour the batter into the bag and twist the top to close it. Cut off the tip of the bag to make a ½-inch opening and pipe out 24 rounds, each 2 inches wide, onto the prepared baking sheets, spacing the rounds at least 1 inch apart.

4 Bake until the cookies are shiny on top and dark golden brown, about 15 minutes. Have an adult help you transfer the cookies to a wire rack and let cool completely.

5 Place another large disposable pastry bag in a container or drinking glass. Transfer the cream cheese frosting into the bag and twist the top to close it. Cut off the tip of the bag to make a ¼-inch opening and pipe about 2 tablespoons frosting onto the flat side of half of the cooled cookies. Top each with a second cookie, flat side down, and press together to spread the frosting to the edge. Store in an airtight container in the refrigerator for up to 2 days.

• •

1½ cups all-purpose flour

1 teaspoon kosher salt

½ teaspoon baking powder

½ teaspoon baking soda

2 tablespoons ground cinnamon

2 teaspoons ground ginger

1 teaspoon ground cloves

1 can (15 oz) pumpkin purée

½ cup vegetable oil

1 large egg

1 teaspoon vanilla extract

1⅓ cups firmly packed dark brown sugar

Cream Cheese Frosting (page 65)

45

Salted Caramel Cinnamon Rolls with Cream Cheese Icing

To save time in the morning, you can prepare the dough ahead and let it rise overnight in the refrigerator. Take it out to let it warm up a bit and rise further while you prepare the caramel filling and the cream cheese icing.

1 In the bowl of a stand mixer, stir together the milk and yeast and let stand until foamy, about 5 minutes. Add the flour, eggs, granulated sugar, salt, and butter. Fit the mixer with the paddle attachment and beat on medium-low speed until combined, about 2 minutes. Switch to the dough hook and beat on low speed until the dough is smooth, about 5 minutes. Transfer the dough to a lightly oiled bowl and cover with plastic wrap. Let rise in a warm spot until doubled in size, about 1 hour.

2 Lightly butter a 10-inch square baking dish. In a small bowl, stir together the brown sugar and cinnamon.

3 Turn the dough out onto a lightly floured work surface and roll out into a 12-by-14-inch rectangle about ¼ inch thick. Spread the caramel filling over the dough, leaving a 1-inch border around the edge. Sprinkle the brown sugar mixture evenly on top. Starting at the long side closest to you, roll the dough into a log and cut crosswise into 12 equal slices. Arrange in rows in the prepared baking dish. Cover with plastic wrap and let rise in a warm spot until doubled in size, about 1 hour. Preheat the oven to 375°F.

4 Bake until the cinnamon rolls are golden brown, about 30 minutes. Have an adult help you transfer the pan to a wire rack and let the rolls cool slightly. Spread the warm rolls with the icing and serve warm.

½ cup warm whole milk (115°F–120°F)

2½ teaspoons active dry yeast

4 cups all-purpose flour, plus more for dusting

4 large eggs

¼ cup granulated sugar

2 teaspoons kosher salt

½ cup unsalted butter, at room temperature, plus more for the pan

2 tablespoons firmly packed light brown sugar

1 teaspoon ground cinnamon

Caramel Filling (page 67)

Cream Cheese Icing (page 66)

Chocolate Almond Orange Biscotti Dipped in Chocolate

In Italy, these crunchy cookies are served alongside steaming cups of strong espresso, foamy cappuccino, or rich hot chocolate—perfect for dunking. Store the biscotti in a glass jar or metal tin to keep them crisp.

1 Preheat the oven to 325°F. Line 2 baking sheets with parchment paper.

2 In a bowl, sift together the flour, baking powder, and salt. Set aside.

3 In the bowl of a stand mixer fitted with the paddle attachment, beat together the butter and sugar on medium speed until light and fluffy, about 3 minutes. Add the eggs 1 at a time, then the orange zest, orange juice, and almond extract, and beat until smooth, about 1 minute.

4 Reduce the speed to low, add the flour mixture, and beat just until the flour mixture disappears, about 3 minutes. Stop the mixer and scrape down the sides of the bowl with a rubber spatula. Add the almonds and one-third of the chopped chocolate and beat until evenly distributed, about 30 seconds.

5 Divide the dough in half and place 1 piece of dough on each prepared baking sheet. Wet your fingertips with cool water to keep the dough from sticking to your hands, then shape each piece of dough into a 10-by-2½-inch log.

2 cups all-purpose flour

1½ teaspoons baking powder

½ teaspoon kosher salt

½ cup unsalted butter, at room temperature

¾ cup sugar

2 large eggs

2 teaspoons grated orange zest

1 tablespoon fresh orange juice

1 teaspoon almond extract

3 oz whole almonds, toasted and chopped into ¼-inch pieces

9 oz semisweet chocolate, chopped into ¼-inch pieces

6 Bake until the logs are golden brown, about 25 minutes. Have an adult help you transfer the baking sheets to a wire rack and let cool until they are safe to handle, about 10 minutes. Transfer the logs to a cutting board. Using a serrated knife, cut the logs crosswise into slices ¾ inch thick. Place the slices, cut side down, on the baking sheets and bake until crisp and golden, 12–14 minutes; halfway through baking, have an adult help you turn the biscotti over.

7 Have an adult help you transfer the baking sheets to a wire rack and let the cookies cool completely on the sheets.

8 Line a baking sheet with clean parchment paper. Put the remaining two-thirds chocolate in a microwave-safe bowl and microwave in 30-second increments, stirring in between, until the chocolate is fully melted and no clumps remain. Dip a flat side of each biscotti into the melted chocolate and place, chocolate side up, on the prepared baking sheet.

9 Let stand until the chocolate is set, about 20 minutes on the countertop or 10 minutes in the refrigerator. Store in an airtight container with parchment or waxed paper between the layers at room temperature for up to 1 week.

Flourless Chocolate Cake

This fudgy, chocolaty cake will be popular with everyone and especially appreciated by those who are trying to avoid gluten in their diets. Using a springform pan will help you remove the cake with ease.

1 Preheat the oven to 375°F. Butter a 9-inch springform pan, line the bottom with parchment paper, and butter the parchment.

2 In a large heatproof bowl, combine the butter and chocolate and set over a saucepan of simmering water, making sure that the water isn't touching the bottom of the bowl. Heat, stirring occasionally, until the butter and chocolate melt, about 5 minutes.

3 Remove the bowl from the heat and whisk in the granulated sugar. Add the eggs 1 at a time and whisk until combined. Stir in the vanilla and the cocoa powder. Pour the batter into the prepared pan and smooth the top.

4 Bake until the top of the cake has formed a thin crust and a toothpick inserted into the center comes out with a few moist crumbs attached, about 25 minutes. Have an adult help you transfer the pan to a wire rack and let cool completely. Loosen the clasp on the pan sides and remove the sides. With the help of a spatula, transfer the cake to a plate.

5 Just before serving, spread the whipped cream over the top of the cooled cake. Using a fine-mesh sieve or a sifter, dust the whipped cream with cocoa powder and confectioners' sugar.

½ cup unsalted butter, plus more for the pan

5 oz semisweet chocolate, coarsely chopped

1¼ cups granulated sugar

3 large eggs

½ teaspoon vanilla extract

½ cup unsweetened cocoa powder, plus more for dusting

Whipped Cream (page 65)

Confectioner's sugar, for dusting

Mini S'mores Tarts with Graham Cracker Crusts

Craving s'mores but can't rustle up a campfire? Here's the solution: s'mores from the kitchen! Watch the marshmallows carefully—they burn just as quickly under the broiler as they do over a campfire.

1 Preheat the oven to 350°F. To make the crust, in a large bowl, stir together the graham crackers, melted butter, and brown sugar. Divide the mixture among 6 mini tart shells or 6 standard muffin cups. Press evenly into the bottoms and up the sides. Place tart shells, if using, on a half sheet pan. Freeze for 15 minutes, then bake until the crusts are set, about 10 minutes. Have an adult help you transfer the pan to a wire rack and let cool completely.

2 To make the filling, in a heatproof bowl, combine the chocolate chips and butter. Set aside. Pour the cream into a small saucepan. Place over medium heat and warm the cream until it just starts to simmer. Carefully pour the cream over the chocolate chips and butter and let stand until the chocolate starts to melt, about 3 minutes, then whisk to combine. Whisk in the granulated sugar and salt.

3 Divide the chocolate mixture evenly among the tart crusts, filling them just below the top edge of the crust. Cover them with plastic wrap and refrigerate for 2 hours or up to 2 days.

4 Just before serving, preheat the broiler. Top the tarts with the miniature marshmallows, dividing evenly, and broil until toasted, about 2 minutes. Let cool before serving. Store in an airtight container in the refrigerator for up to 2 days.

For the crust

9 graham crackers, finely crushed

6 tablespoons unsalted butter, melted and cooled

2 tablespoons firmly packed dark brown sugar

For the filling

1 cup milk chocolate chips

2 tablespoons unsalted butter, at room temperature

½ cup heavy cream

1 tablespoon granulated sugar

½ teaspoon kosher salt

1½ cups miniature marshmallows

Cheddar Bacon Scones

Try splitting these scones and topping them with apple butter or thinly sliced apples. The sweet-tart fruit provides a counterpoint to the salty and savory flavors of the scones.

1 Preheat the oven to 400°F. Line 2 baking sheets with parchment paper.

2 In a food processor, combine the flour, baking powder, baking soda, salt, and pepper and pulse until blended. Add the butter and process until the mixture resembles coarse sand. In a small bowl, whisk together the egg and buttermilk. With the processor running, add the egg mixture in a slow, steady stream and process until the dough just comes together.

3 Transfer the dough to a large bowl and use a rubber spatula to fold in the cheese, bacon, and chives. Turn the dough out onto a well-floured work surface and divide in half. Form each half into a round about 8 inches in diameter and 1 inch thick. Cut each round into 8 wedges. Place on the prepared baking sheets, spacing the scones about 1 inch apart.

4 Bake until the scones are golden brown, about 15 minutes. Have an adult help you transfer the scones to a wire rack and let cool completely. Store in an airtight container at room temperature for up to 3 days.

2 cups all-purpose flour, plus more for dusting

2 teaspoons baking powder

½ teaspoon baking soda

1 teaspoon kosher salt

½ teaspoon freshly ground pepper

½ cup cold unsalted butter, cut into cubes

1 large egg

¾ cup buttermilk

1 cup grated Cheddar cheese

½ lb cooked bacon, finely chopped

1 tablespoon finely chopped fresh chives

Buttermilk Biscuits with Herb Butter

A platter of crispy fried chicken is a perfect accompaniment for these biscuits. If you have leftover herb butter, use it as a spread for crunchy cucumber sandwiches on rye or sourdough bread.

1 To make the biscuits, preheat the oven to 375°F. Line a baking sheet with parchment paper.

2 In a large bowl, whisk together the flour, salt, baking powder, and baking soda. Add the butter and toss to coat with the flour. Working quickly with a pastry blender or 2 knives, cut the butter into the flour mixture until pea-size pieces form. Add the buttermilk and cream and stir until a wet, shaggy dough forms.

3 Turn the dough out onto a generously floured work surface and dust the top of the dough with flour. Knead once or twice until the dough comes together. Using floured hands, pat the dough into a round about 1 inch thick. Dip a 2-inch round cutter in flour and cut out as many biscuits as you can; be sure to press the cutter straight down into the dough without twisting. Transfer to the prepared baking sheet, spacing the biscuits at least 1 inch apart. Gather the scraps into a ball, pat into another 1-inch-thick round, and cut out more biscuits.

4 Bake until the biscuits have risen and are golden brown, about 20 minutes. Have an adult help you transfer the biscuits to a wire rack and let cool slightly.

5 Meanwhile, make the herb butter: In a small bowl, mix together the butter, rosemary, and thyme and season with salt and pepper. Stir until blended. Serve the biscuits warm with the herb butter. Store in an airtight container at room temperature for up to 3 days.

For the biscuits

2 cups all-purpose flour, plus more for dusting

1½ teaspoons kosher salt

1½ teaspoons baking powder

½ teaspoon baking soda

½ cup cold unsalted butter, cut into pieces

½ cup cold buttermilk

½ cup cold heavy cream

For the herb butter

½ cup unsalted butter, at room temperature

1 tablespoon minced fresh rosemary

2 teaspoons minced fresh thyme

Kosher salt and freshly ground pepper

Focaccia topped with Tomatoes, Thyme & Parmesan

Like the pizza dough it resembles, you can top focaccia with almost anything you fancy. Try thinly sliced potatoes brushed with olive oil and sprinkled with fresh rosemary—a classic combination popular in Florence, Italy.

1 In the bowl of a stand mixer, stir together the yeast, sugar, kosher salt, and warm water, then stir in ¼ cup of the flour. Let stand until foamy, about 5 minutes. Add the remaining 2¾ cups flour, fit the mixer with the paddle attachment, and beat on low speed until the dough starts to come together, about 1 minute. Switch to the dough hook and beat on low speed until the dough forms a smooth, elastic ball, about 5 minutes.

2 Transfer the dough to a lightly oiled bowl and cover with plastic wrap. Let the dough rise at room temperature until doubled in size, about 1½ hours.

3 Line a quarter sheet pan with parchment paper and brush the parchment with 1 tablespoon of the oil. Punch down the dough, then turn it out onto the prepared pan and stretch it to fit the pan. Cover loosely with plastic wrap and let rise in a warm spot until doubled in size, about 30 minutes.

1½ teaspoons active dry yeast

½ teaspoon sugar

½ teaspoon kosher salt

1 cup warm water (110°F–115°F)

3 cups all-purpose flour

4 tablespoons olive oil, plus more for the bowl

1 tablespoon coarsely chopped fresh thyme

1 cup cherry tomatoes, halved

½ cup grated Parmesan cheese

Flaky sea salt, for sprinkling

4 Meanwhile, preheat the oven to 425°F. Using your fingertips, make a pattern of dimples over the entire surface of the dough, spacing them about 2 inches apart. Drizzle with 2 tablespoons of the oil, sprinkle with ½ tablespoon of the thyme, and arrange the tomatoes on top. Drizzle the remaining 1 tablespoon oil over the tomatoes and sprinkle with the remaining ½ tablespoon thyme.

5 Bake until the edges of the focaccia are golden brown and a toothpick inserted into the center comes out dry, 20–25 minutes. Have an adult help you remove the pan from the oven. Sprinkle the cheese over the focaccia and bake until just melted, about 2 minutes longer. Let the focaccia cool slightly in the pan before serving. Sprinkle with sea salt and cut into slices. Store slices in an airtight container at room temperature for up to 3 days.

You can also add thin slices of red onion or pitted, sliced olives in place of or along with the cherry tomatoes.

Cheesy Crackers

Impress your friends and family with homemade crackers. They'll never guess how easy they are to make, plus they taste better than any fancy store-bought versions! Refrigerating the dough makes the log easier to slice into neat rounds for baking.

1 In a food processor, combine both cheeses, the butter, flour, and cayenne and process until well combined and crumbly, 40–60 seconds. Transfer the dough to a sheet of plastic wrap and shape into a log about 2 inches in diameter and 6–7 inches long. Roll up the log in the plastic wrap, patting it to form a smooth, even cylinder. Refrigerate for at least 1 hour or up to overnight.

2 Preheat the oven to 350°F. Unwrap the dough and slice into rounds about ¼ inch thick. Arrange on 2 ungreased rimmed baking sheets, preferably nonstick, spacing the rounds about 2 inches apart. Sprinkle each round with a pinch of salt.

3 Bake the crackers, 1 sheet at a time, until light golden brown, 10–15 minutes; halfway through baking, have an adult help you rotate the pan 180 degrees. For crispier crackers, bake for up to 3 minutes longer, watching carefully to avoid over-browning. Let the crackers cool completely on the baking sheet. Store in an airtight container for up to 3 days.

2 cups shredded Cheddar or Gruyère cheese

½ cup grated Parmesan cheese

6 tablespoons cold unsalted butter, cut into pieces

1 cup all-purpose flour

Pinch of cayenne pepper

Sea salt, for sprinkling

Lemon Poppy Seed Loaf with Lemon Glaze

The yogurt in this recipe is a healthy alternative to butter and, along with the lemon, gives the bread a tart and tangy flavor. Try spreading another dollop of thick, creamy yogurt on a slice when it is warm from the oven.

1 Preheat the oven to 350°F. Grease a 9-by-5-inch loaf pan with nonstick cooking spray.

2 In a medium bowl, whisk together the flour, poppy seeds, baking powder, and salt. In a large bowl, whisk together the yogurt, granulated sugar, eggs, lemon zest, 2 tablespoons of the lemon juice, the vanilla, and oil. Add the flour mixture to the yogurt mixture and whisk just until the flour mixture disappears. Pour the batter into the prepared pan and smooth the top.

3 Bake until the bread is golden brown and a toothpick inserted into the center comes out with just a few moist crumbs attached, about 1 hour. Have an adult help you transfer the pan to a wire rack and let cool slightly. Then turn the loaf out onto the rack to cool completely.

4 Meanwhile, in a small bowl, whisk together the confectioners' sugar and the remaining 4 tablespoons lemon juice. Pour the glaze over the cooled loaf and let set for about 5 minutes before slicing. Store the loaf wrapped in plastic wrap at room temperature for up to 2 days.

Nonstick cooking spray

1½ cups all-purpose flour

2 tablespoons poppy seeds

2 teaspoons baking powder

¾ teaspoon kosher salt

1 cup plain full-fat Greek yogurt

1 cup granulated sugar

3 large eggs

2 teaspoons grated lemon zest

6 tablespoons fresh lemon juice

1 teaspoon vanilla extract

½ cup vegetable oil

1 cup confectioners' sugar

"Everything Bagel" Parker House Rolls

The original recipe was developed almost 150 years ago, but the zesty bagel-inspired topping brings it up-to-date. These fluffy rolls are perfect for soaking up gravy or simply serving with butter.

1 To make the rolls, in a large measuring cup, combine the milk, sugar, and yeast. Let stand until foamy, about 5 minutes. Transfer the yeast mixture to the bowl of a stand mixer fitted with the paddle attachment. Add the 4 tablespoons butter, the flour, and kosher salt and beat on low speed just until the flour disappears, about 1 minute. Switch to the dough hook and beat on medium-low speed until the dough is smooth and elastic, about 5 minutes.

2 Transfer the dough to a lightly oiled bowl and cover with plastic wrap. Let the dough rise in a warm spot until doubled in size, about 1 hour.

3 Butter an 8-inch square baking dish. Transfer the dough to a floured surface, divide it into 16 equal pieces, and roll each into a ball. Arrange the balls of dough in the baking dish in 4 rows of 4. Cover tightly with plastic wrap; let rise in a warm spot until doubled in size, about 30 minutes.

4 Meanwhile, preheat the oven to 375°F. To make the seasoning, in a small bowl, stir together the sea salt, sesame seeds, poppy seeds, onion flakes, and garlic flakes. Brush the tops of the rolls with the melted butter and sprinkle with the sea salt mixture.

5 Bake until the rolls are golden on top and puffed up, 18–20 minutes. Have an adult help you transfer the baking dish to a wire rack and let cool slightly, then invert the rolls onto the rack. Serve warm.

For the rolls

1 cup warm whole milk (115°F–120°F)

2 tablespoons sugar

2½ teaspoons active dry yeast

4 tablespoons unsalted butter, at room temperature, plus 2 tablespoons melted and cooled, and butter for the dish

3 cups all-purpose flour, plus more for dusting

1½ teaspoons kosher salt

For the seasoning

1½ teaspoons flaky sea salt

1 teaspoon white sesame seeds

1 teaspoon poppy seeds

½ teaspoon dried onion flakes

½ teaspoon dried garlic flakes

Who can resist
cream cheese frosting!
For a festive touch,
sprinkle the cupcakes
with small red
sprinkles.

Whipped Cream

MAKES 3 CUPS

1½ cups heavy cream

¼ cup confectioners' sugar, plus more for dusting

½ teaspoon vanilla extract

In the bowl of a stand mixer fitted with the whisk attachment, beat together the cream, confectioners' sugar, and vanilla on medium speed until light and fluffy, about 3 minutes.

Cookies & Cream Frosting

MAKES 3 CUPS

¾ cup unsalted butter, at room temperature

Pinch of kosher salt

1½ cups confectioners' sugar, sifted

¾ cup finely ground chocolate sandwich cookies

In the bowl of a stand mixer fitted with the paddle attachment, beat together the butter and salt on medium-high speed until smooth, about 2 minutes. Reduce the speed to medium, add the confectioners' sugar, ¼ cup at a time, and beat until light and fluffy, about 2 minutes. Stop the mixer and scrape down the sides of the bowl as needed. Reduce the speed to low, add the ground cookies, and beat until combined, about 30 seconds.

Cream Cheese Frosting

MAKES 2 CUPS

½ cup unsalted butter, at room temperature

1 package (½ lb) cream cheese, at room temperature

3 cups confectioners' sugar, sifted

1½ teaspoons vanilla extract

1 tablespoon whole milk or heavy cream

Pinch of kosher salt

In the bowl of a stand mixer fitted with the paddle attachment, beat together the butter and cream cheese on medium-high speed until smooth, about 2 minutes. Add the confectioners' sugar, vanilla, milk, and salt and beat on medium speed until well combined, about 3 minutes. Raise the speed to high and beat until fluffy and combined, about 30 seconds.

Buttercream Frosting

MAKES 4 CUPS

In the bowl of a stand mixer fitted with the paddle attachment, beat the butter on medium-high speed until light and fluffy, about 2 minutes. Add the confectioners' sugar in 2 additions, then add the vanilla and beat until smooth, about 1 minute. Add the cream and beat until thick and creamy, about 3 minutes.

1 cup unsalted butter, at room temperature

6 cups confectioners' sugar

1 tablespoon vanilla extract

¼ cup heavy cream

Cream Cheese Icing

MAKES 2 CUPS

In the bowl of a stand mixer fitted with the paddle attachment, beat together the butter, cream cheese, confectioners' sugar, and vanilla on low speed until combined, about 4 minutes. Raise the speed to high and beat until smooth, about 1 minute.

4 tablespoons unsalted butter, at room temperature

1 package (½ lb) cream cheese, at room temperature

1 cup confectioners' sugar

2 teaspoons vanilla extract

Cream Cheese Dough

MAKES 16 SERVINGS

In a food processor, combine the flour, butter, and cream cheese and process until combined and a dough forms. Turn the dough out onto a floured work surface and shape into a disk. Wrap in plastic wrap and refrigerate for 15 minutes before rolling out. The dough can be frozen for up to 1 month; defrost in the refrigerator for 12 hours before using.

3 cups all-purpose flour, plus more for dusting

1 cup cold unsalted butter, cut into cubes

1 package (½ lb) cream cheese, at room temperature

Chocolate Tart Dough

In a small bowl, whisk together the egg yolk, vanilla, and 3 tablespoons water. Set aside.

In a food processor, pulse the hazelnuts a few times until broken up. Add the flour, sugar, and salt and process until combined. Add the butter and process until the mixture resembles coarse sand. With the processor running, add the egg yolk mixture and process until a dough forms.

Transfer the dough to a 10-inch tart pan and press evenly into the bottom and up the sides of the pan. Freeze for 15 minutes before baking or freeze for up to 1 month before using.

1 large egg yolk

1 teaspoon vanilla extract

½ cup hazelnuts

1¼ cups all-purpose flour

⅓ cup sugar

¼ teaspoon kosher salt

½ cup cold unsalted butter, cut into cubes

Caramel Filling

In a small saucepan, combine the brown sugar and butter. Place over medium heat and cook, stirring occasionally, until the color deepens, about 5 minutes. Remove from the heat, carefully add the cream and salt, and stir to combine. Transfer to a medium bowl and let cool to room temperature.

½ cup firmly packed light brown sugar

4 tablespoons unsalted butter

¼ cup heavy cream

1 teaspoon kosher salt

Salted Caramel Chocolate Chip Cookies

MAKES 24 COOKIES

Perfect Chocolate Chip Cookies (page 20)
12 salted caramel candies

Make the cookie dough as directed and scoop into 1½-tablespoon rounds. Cut the caramel candies in half. Press a caramel half into the center of each round and press the dough together to completely enclose the caramel. Roll into a ball and bake as directed, increasing the bake time to 10–12 minutes.

Brown Butter & Hazelnut Blondies

MAKES 12-16 BARS

1 cup unsalted butter
Brown Sugar Blondies (page 39), without the ¾ cup butter
⅔ cup hazelnuts, coarsely chopped

In a large sauté pan over medium heat, melt the butter. Reduce the heat to medium-low and simmer gently, swirling the pan often, until the butter is toasty brown and smells nutty, 5–7 minutes. Watch carefully at the end to prevent the butter from burning. Transfer to a bowl and let cool to room temperature. Refrigerate until it is the consistency of softened butter, about 30 minutes. Make the blondie batter as directed, replacing the ¾ cup butter with the brown butter. Fold the hazelnuts with the white chocolate chips and bake as directed.

Strawberry Topping

MAKES 2⅓ CUPS

1 lb strawberries, hulled and sliced
1 tablespoon fresh lemon juice
3 tablespoons sugar

In a bowl, stir together the strawberries, lemon juice, and sugar. Let sit for at least 5 minutes, until the strawberries begin to release some juices. Use as a topping or serve with Whipped Cream (page 65).

Index

A

Almonds
  Chocolate Almond Orange
    Biscotti Dipped in
    Chocolate, 48–49
  Dried Cherry & Almond
    Mini Scones, 43
Apple Hand Pies, 27

B

Baking powder, 11
Baking soda, 11
Bananas
  Banana-Butterscotch
    Pie, 30
  Chocolate Banana
    Loaf Bread, 15
Bar cookies
  Brown Butter Rice
    Krispy Treats, 38
  Brown Sugar Blondies, 39
  Brown Butter & Hazelnut
    Blondies, 68
  Millionaire's
    Shortbread, 35–36
  Nutella Brownies, 31
Berry, Mixed, Mini Galettes, 12
Biscuits & Rolls
  Buttermilk Biscuits with
    Herb Butter, 55
  "Everything Bagel"
    Parker House Rolls, 62
  Salted Caramel Cinnamon
    Rolls with Cream
    Cheese Icing, 46
Breads. See also Biscuits
  & Rolls; Scones
  Chocolate Banana
    Bread Loaf, 15
  Cinnamon Monkey
    Bread, 16–17

Coffee-Cake Muffins, 21
Focaccia Topped with
  Tomatoes, Thyme &
  Parmesan, 56–57
Lemon Poppy Seed Loaf
  with Lemon Glaze, 61
Buttercream Frosting, 66
Buttermilk, substitute for, 11
Buttermilk Biscuits with
  Herb Butter, 55

C

Cakes. See also Cupcakes
  Confetti Birthday
    Cake, 41–42
  Flourless Chocolate
    Cake, 51
Caramel
  Caramel Filling, 67
  Salted Caramel Chocolate
    Chip Cookies, 68
  Salted Caramel Cinnamon
    Rolls with Cream
    Cheese Icing, 46
Cheddar Bacon Scones, 54
Cheese. See also Cream
  Cheese
  Cheddar Bacon
    Scones, 54
  Cheesy Crackers, 60
  Focaccia Topped with
    Tomatoes, Thyme
    & Parmesan, 56–57
Cheesecake, Vanilla,
  with Strawberries, 22
Cherry, Dried, & Almond
  Mini Scones, 43
Chocolate
  Chocolate Almond
    Orange Biscotti Dipped
    in Chocolate, 48–49

Chocolate Banana
  Loaf Bread, 15
Chocolate Tart Dough, 67
Chocolate Tart with
  Crushed Hazelnuts, 37
Cookies & Cream
  Frosting, 65
Flourless Chocolate
  Cake, 51
Millionaire's
  Shortbread, 35–36
Mini S'mores Tarts
  with Graham Cracker
  Crusts, 52
Nutella Brownies, 31
Perfect Chocolate Chip
  Cookies, 20
Salted Caramel Chocolate
  Chip Cookies, 68
Cinnamon
  Cinnamon Monkey
    Bread, 16–17
  Salted Caramel Cinnamon
    Rolls with Cream
    Cheese Frosting, 46
Coffee-Cake Muffins, 21
Confetti Birthday
  Cake, 41–42
Cookies
  Chocolate Almond
    Orange Biscotti Dipped
    in Chocolate, 48–49
  Madeleines, 24
  Perfect Chocolate Chip
    Cookies, 20
  Salted Caramel Chocolate
    Chip Cookies, 68
Cookies & Cream
  Frosting, 65
Cookies & Cream Mini
  Cupcakes, 25

Cream Cheese
  Cream Cheese Dough, 66
  Cream Cheese
    Frosting, 65
  Cream Cheese Icing, 66
  Vanilla Cheesecake
    with Strawberries, 22
Cupcakes
  Cookies & Cream Mini
    Cupcakes, 25
  Red Velvet Cupcakes, 28

E

Eggs, size and substitutes
  for, 11
Equipment, preparing, 8
"Everything Bagel"
  Parker House Rolls, 62

F

Flour, 11
Flourless Chocolate
  Cake, 51
Focaccia Topped
  with Tomatoes, Thyme
  & Parmesan, 56-57
Frostings
  Buttercream Frosting, 66
  Cookies & Cream
    Frosting, 65
  Cream Cheese
    Frosting, 65
Fruit, dried, substituting, 11

H

Hazelnuts
  Brown Butter & Hazelnut
    Blondies, 68
  Chocolate Tart with
    Crushed Hazelnuts, 37

I

Icing, Cream Cheese, 66
Ingredients, 11

L

Lemon Poppy Seed Loaf
  with Lemon Glaze, 61

M

Madeleines, 24
Marshmallows
  Brown Butter Rice
    Krispy Treats, 38
  Mini S'mores Tarts
    with Graham Cracker
    Crusts, 52
Meringues, Raspberry
  Swirled, 32
Muffins, Coffee-Cake, 21

N

Nutella Brownies, 31
Nuts, substituting, 11

P

Pastry dough
  Chocolate Tart Dough, 67
  Cream Cheese Dough, 66
Pies
  Apple Hand Pies, 27
  Banana-Butterscotch
    Pie, 30
  Mixed Berry Mini
    Galettes, 12
Pumpkin Whoopie Pies, 45

R

Raspberry Swirled
  Meringues, 32
Red Velvet Cupcakes, 28
Rice Krispy Treats,
  Brown Butter, 38

S

Scones
  Cheddar Bacon
    Scones, 54
  Dried Cherry & Almond
    Mini Scones, 43
Strawberries
  Strawberry Topping, 68
  Vanilla Cheesecake
    with Strawberries, 22

T

Tarts
  Chocolate Tart with
    Crushed Hazelnuts, 37
  Mini S'mores Tarts with
    Graham Cracker
    Crusts, 52
Tomatoes, Thyme
  & Parmesan, Focaccia
  Topped with, 56-57

V

Vanilla Cheesecake
  with Strawberries, 22
Vanilla extract, pure, 11

W

Whipped Cream, 65
Whoopie Pies,
  Pumpkin, 45

THE JUNIOR BAKER COOKBOOK

Conceived and produced by Weldon Owen International
In collaboration with Williams Sonoma, Inc.
3250 Van Ness Avenue, San Francisco, CA 94109

A WELDON OWEN PRODUCTION

PO Box 3088

San Rafael, CA 94912

www.weldonowen.com

Printed in China

First printed in 2017

10 9 8 7 6

Library of Congress Cataloging-in-Publication
data is available.

ISBN: 978-1-68188-267-3

WELDON OWEN INTERNATIONAL

President & Publisher Roger Shaw

SVP, Sales & Marketing Amy Kaneko

Associate Publisher Amy Marr
Associate Editor Emma Rudolph

Creative Director Kelly Booth
Art Director Marisa Kwek
Associate Art Director Lisa Berman
Senior Production Designer Rachel Lopez Metzger

Associate Production Director Michelle Duggan

Imaging Manager Don Hill

Photographer Aubrie Pick
Food Stylist Jen Straus
Prop Stylist Kerrie Sherrell Walsh

ACKNOWLEDGMENTS

Weldon Owen wishes to thank the following people for their generous support
in producing this book: Kris Balloun, Lesley Bruynesteyn, Gloria Geller,
Amy Hatwig, Jalen Hennessy, Josephine Hsu, Alexa Hyman, Bessma Khalaf,
Heidi Ladendorf, Amarech Mendez, Elizabeth Parson, Kristen Tate, and Genesis Vallejo.